FOR MY HUSBAND FRANK

MY FATHER KIM KWAN KEOM

AND MY MOTHER KANG CHUN SUN

Uijung Kim is a Korean illustrator living and working in Brooklyn.
Her work is inspired by childhood experiences and is deeply rooted in Korean culture.
Her clients include *The New York Times*, Facebook, PLANADVISER, and Scholastic.

UNDERGROUND

Conceived and illustrated by Uijung Kim

British Library Cataloguing-in-Publication Data.

A CIP record for this book is available from the British Library.
ISBN: 978-1-908714-83-1
First published: United Kingdom, 2019; United States, 2020.
This edition published 2022.

Cicada Books Ltd
48 Burghley Road
London, NW5 1UE
www.cicadabooks.co.uk

© Cicada Books Limited

UNDERGROUND

SUBWAY SYSTEMS AROUND THE WORLD

UIJUNG KIM

CONTENTS

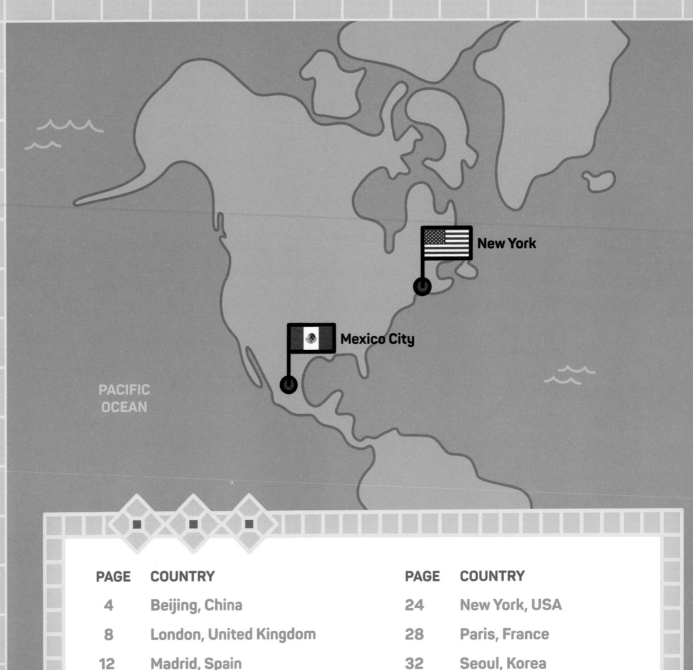

New York

Mexico City

PACIFIC
OCEAN

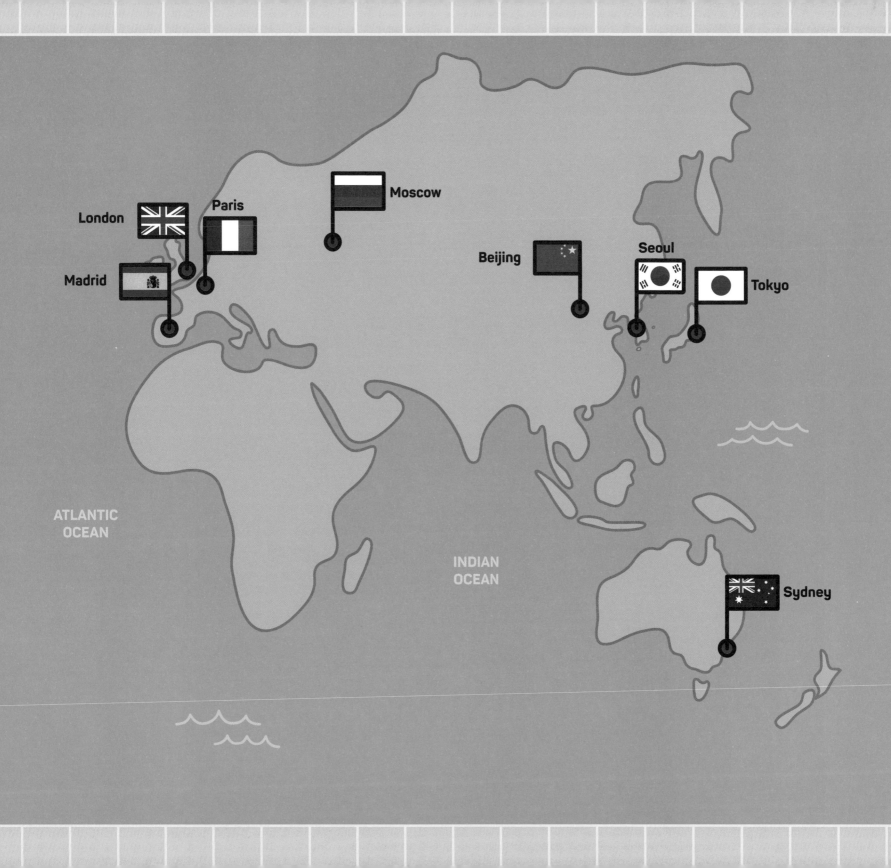

BEIJING

10 MILLION RIDERS EVERY DAY

31 MI THE LENGTH OF THE BEIJING SUBWAY IN 2001

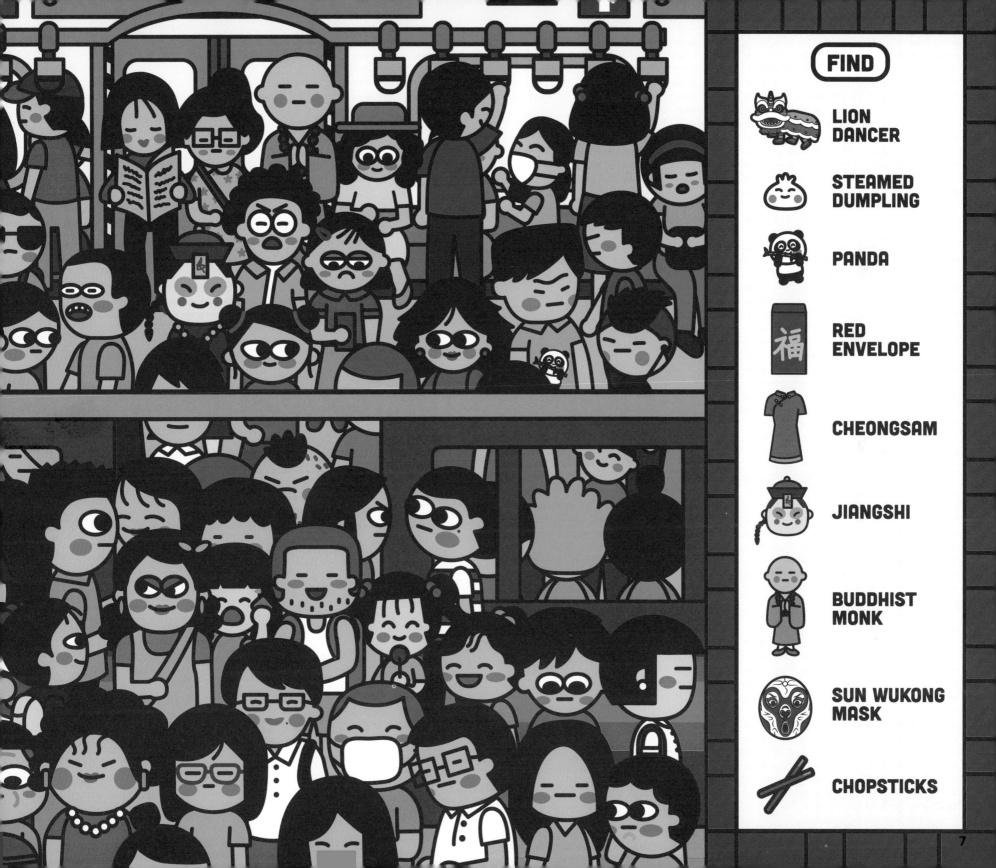

FIND

- LION DANCER
- STEAMED DUMPLING
- PANDA
- RED ENVELOPE
- CHEONGSAM
- JIANGSHI
- BUDDHIST MONK
- SUN WUKONG MASK
- CHOPSTICKS

LONDON

1863
DATE OPENED

1890
THE YEAR
IT BECAME KNOWN
AS 'THE TUBE' DUE TO
THE SHAPE OF THE
TUNNELS

192FT
THE DEEPEST
STATION AT
HAMPSTEAD

233
ALDGATE
CIRCLE LINE

21427

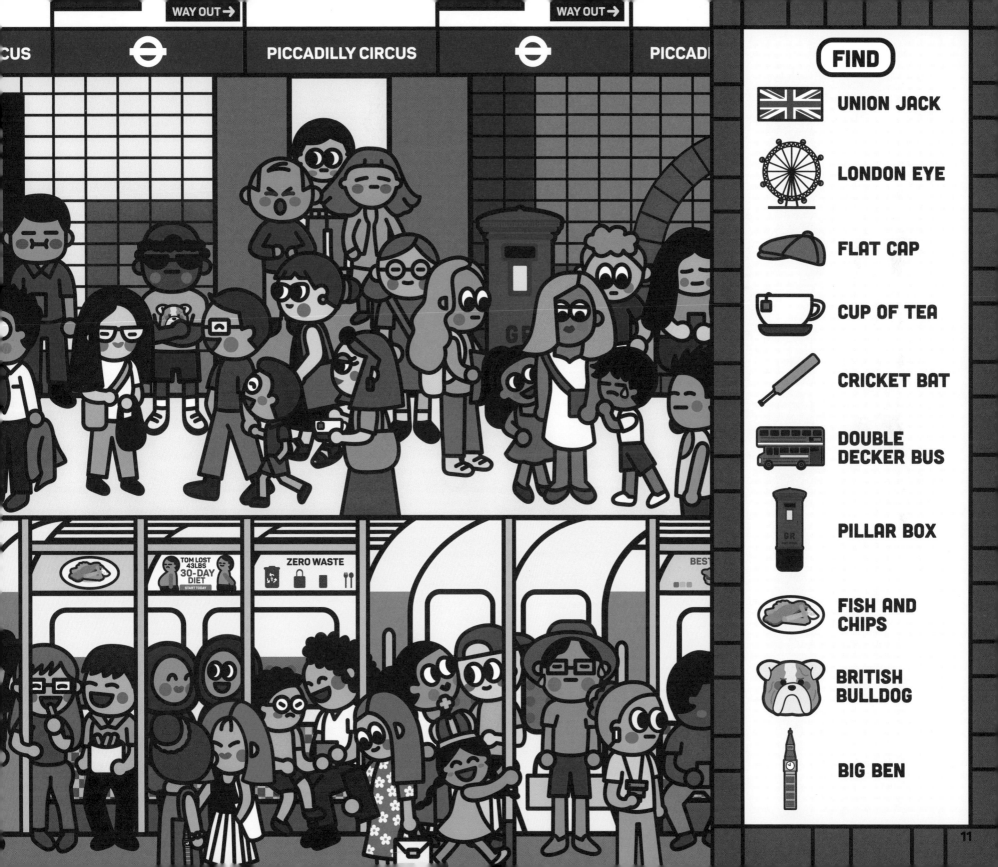

← Salida

MADRID

12TH LONGEST SUBWAY SYSTEM IN THE WORLD

◄Metro►

302 STATIONS

182 MI OF TRACK

13 LINES

← Salida

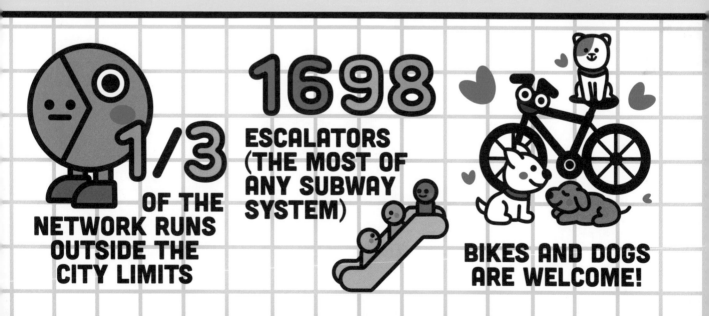

1/3 OF THE NETWORK RUNS OUTSIDE THE CITY LIMITS

1698 ESCALATORS (THE MOST OF ANY SUBWAY SYSTEM)

BIKES AND DOGS ARE WELCOME!

MEXICO CITY

PANTITLAN

026

METRO **STC** SISTEMA DE TRANSPORTE COLECTIVO IS THE OFFICIAL NAME FOR THE MEXICO CITY SUBWAY

1.662 BILLION PASSENGERS PER YEAR

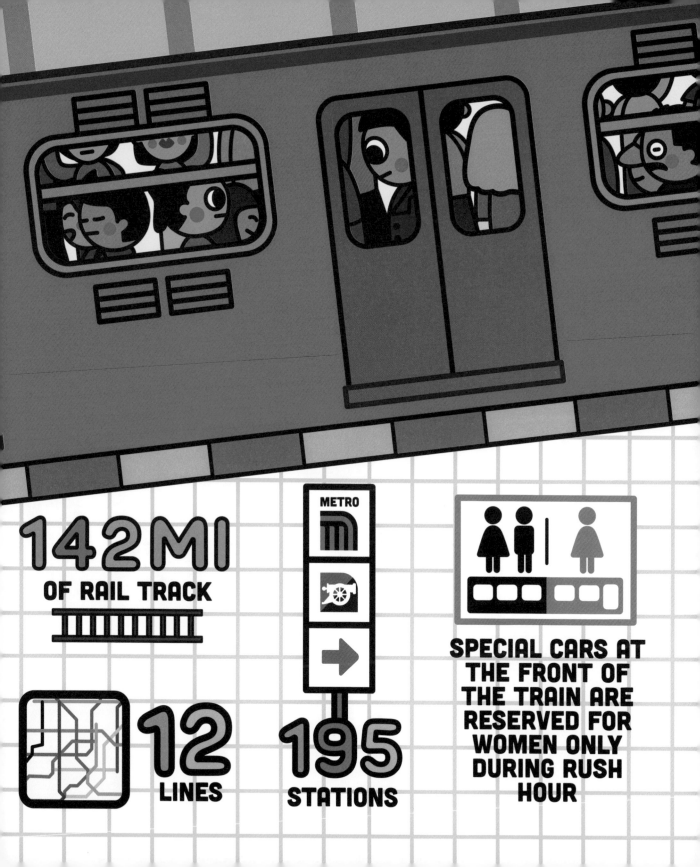

142MI
OF RAIL TRACK

12
LINES

METRO

195
STATIONS

SPECIAL CARS AT THE FRONT OF THE TRAIN ARE RESERVED FOR WOMEN ONLY DURING RUSH HOUR

FRIDA KAHLO

FIND

SAGUARO CACTUS

PIÑATA

LUCHA LIBRE MASK

MARACAS

SOMBRERO DE CHARRO

CHICHEN ITZA

TACO

PAPEL PICADO

CALAVERA

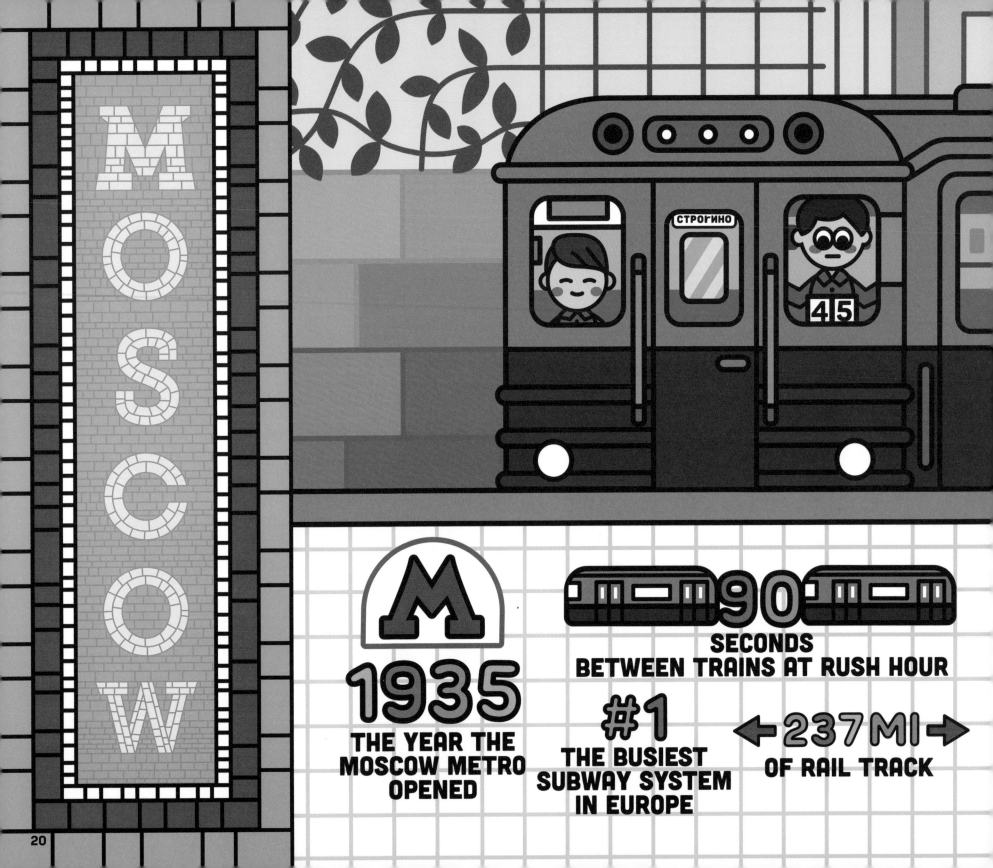

MOSCOW

1935
THE YEAR THE
MOSCOW METRO
OPENED

90
SECONDS
BETWEEN TRAINS AT RUSH HOUR

#1
THE BUSIEST
SUBWAY SYSTEM
IN EUROPE

←**237MI**→
OF RAIL TRACK

СТРОГИНО

45

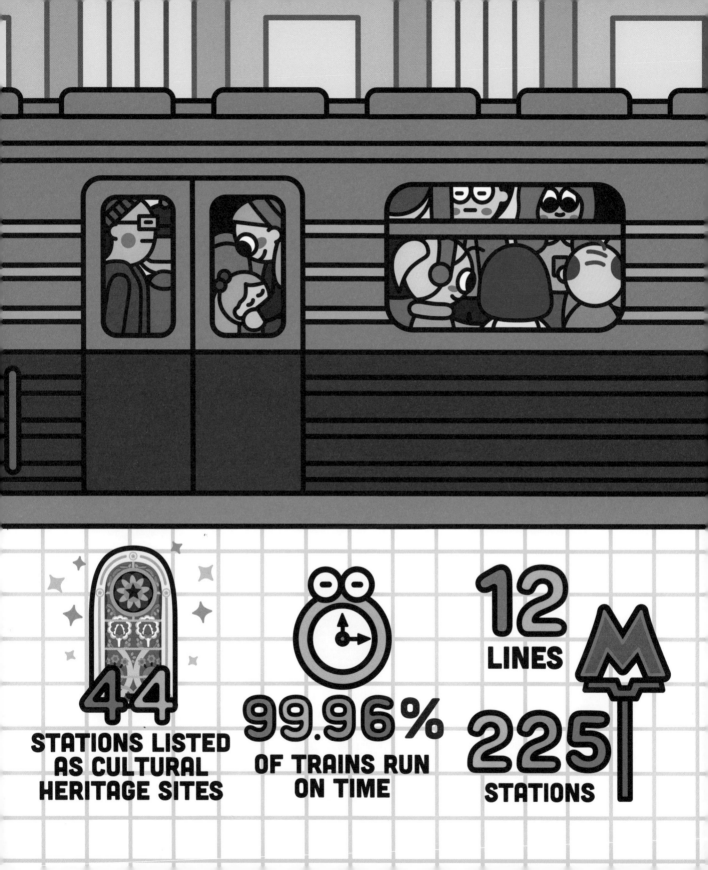

44
STATIONS LISTED
AS CULTURAL
HERITAGE SITES

99.96%
OF TRAINS RUN
ON TIME

12
LINES

225
STATIONS

FIND

DOUBLE HEADED EAGLE

ST BASIL'S CATHEDRAL

RUSSIAN BEAR

KHLEB-SOL

VALENKI BOOTS

FABERGÉ EGG

BALALAIKA

MATRYOSHKA DOLL

BALLERINA

23

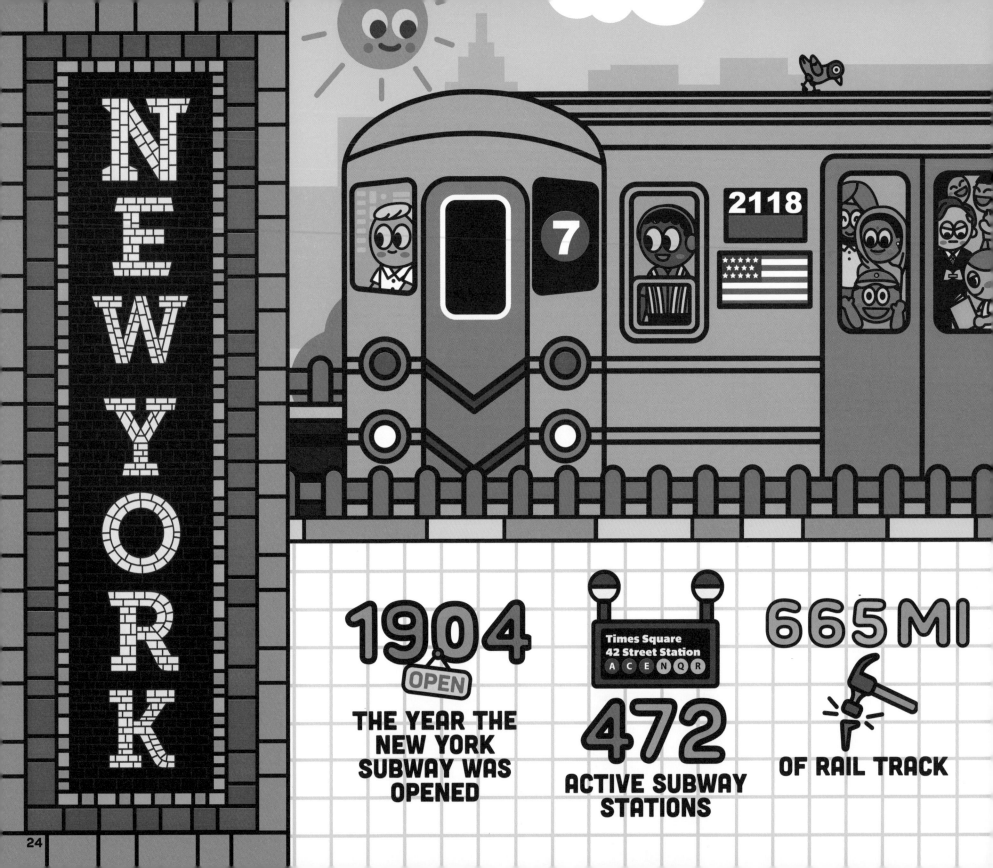

NEW YORK

2118

7

1904
OPEN
THE YEAR THE NEW YORK SUBWAY WAS OPENED

Times Square
42 Street Station
A C E N Q R

472
ACTIVE SUBWAY STATIONS

665 MI
OF RAIL TRACK

48MI
THE LENGTH OF
THE LONGEST
LINE, THE A-TRAIN

180FT
THE DEEPEST
SUBWAY STATION
AT 191ST STREET

57
MILLION
RIDES TAKEN
EVERY DAY

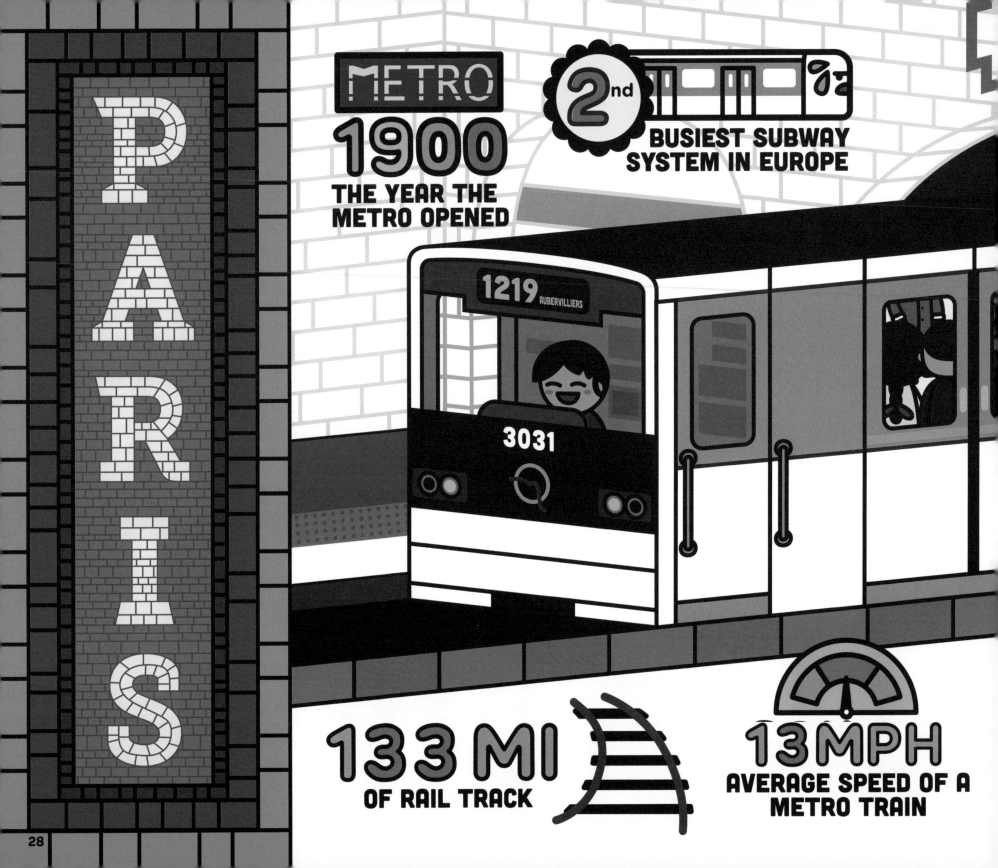

PARIS

METRO

1900
THE YEAR THE
METRO OPENED

2nd
BUSIEST SUBWAY
SYSTEM IN EUROPE

1219 AUBERVILLIERS

3031

133 MI
OF RAIL TRACK

13 MPH
AVERAGE SPEED OF A
METRO TRAIN

ARTS ET MÉTIERS

BONJOUR!

FIND

EIFFEL TOWER

CAMEMBERT

CROISSANT

MACARON

BRETON TOP

MOUSTACHE

BERET

BAGUETTE

SCOOTER

31

SEOUL

1974
THE YEAR
THE FIRST LINE
OPENED

10
NEW SUBWAY
LINES TO OPEN
BY 2025

205 MI
OF RAIL TRACK

291
STATIONS

지하철
SUBWAY
강남
Gangnam

Innner
Circle Line 2156

2913

YEOKSAM STATION 역삼 221 GANGNAM STATION 강남 222 → SEOUL NATIONAL UNIVERSITY -OF EDUCATION STATION 교대 223

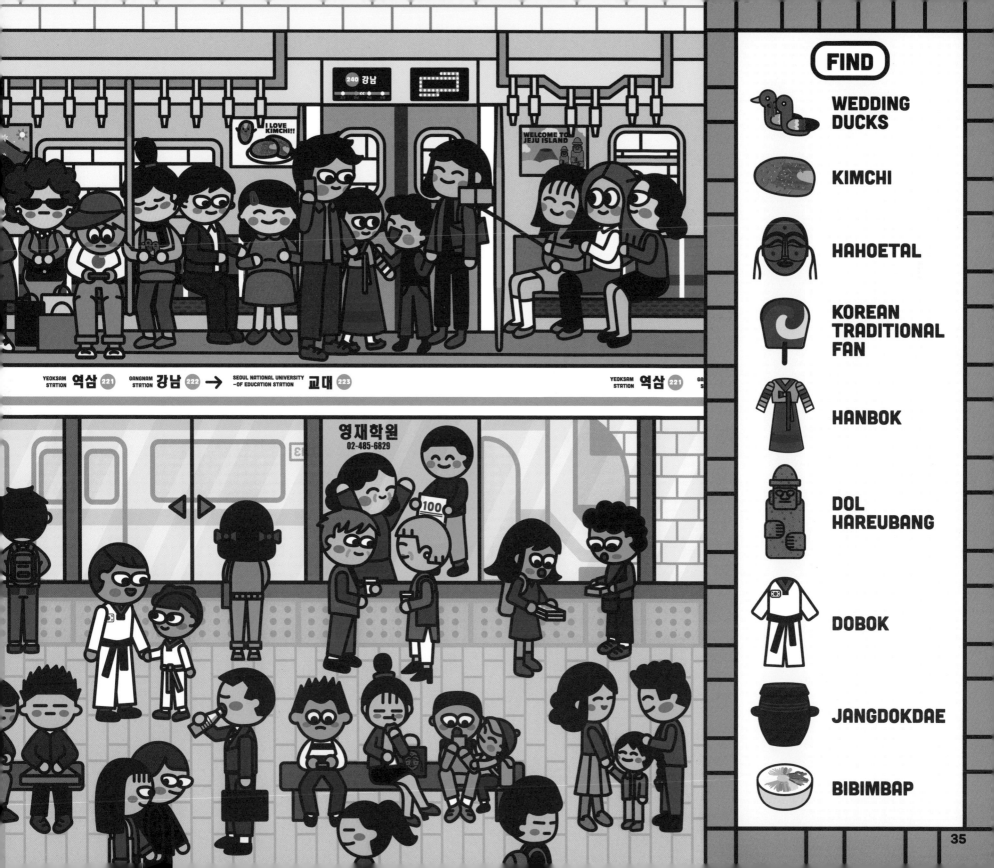

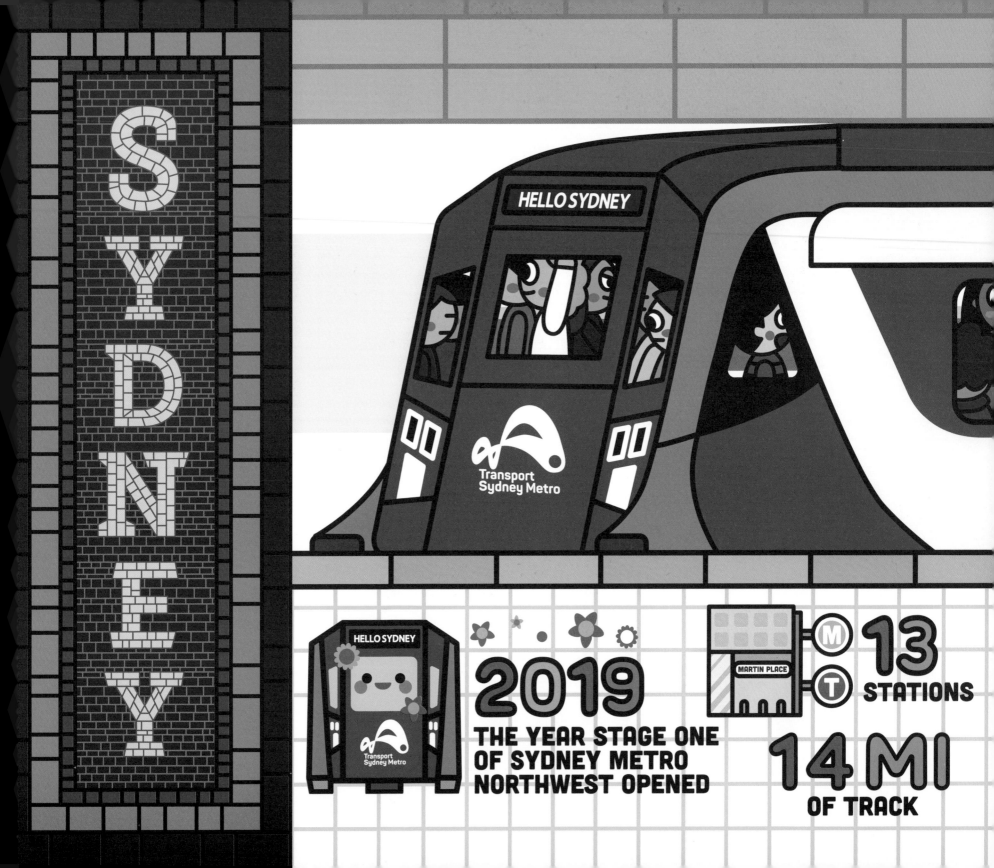

SYDNEY

HELLO SYDNEY

Transport
Sydney Metro

HELLO SYDNEY

Transport
Sydney Metro

2019
THE YEAR STAGE ONE
OF SYDNEY METRO
NORTHWEST OPENED

MARTIN PLACE

Ⓜ Ⓣ **13**
STATIONS

14 MI
OF TRACK

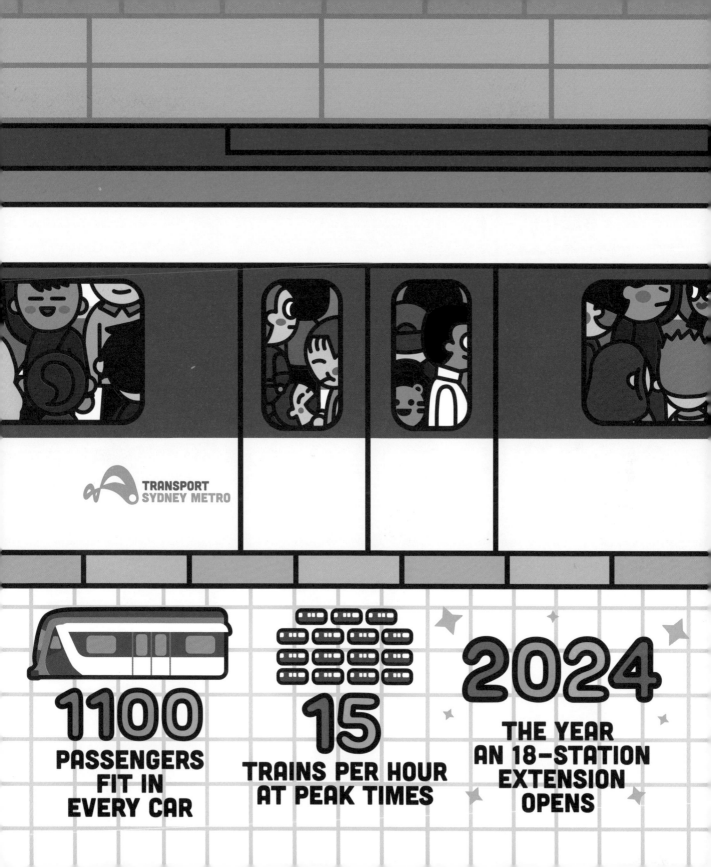

TRANSPORT SYDNEY METRO

1100
PASSENGERS FIT IN EVERY CAR

15
TRAINS PER HOUR AT PEAK TIMES

2024
THE YEAR AN 18-STATION EXTENSION OPENS

FIND

SYDNEY OPERA HOUSE

KOALA

SYDNEY HARBOUR BRIDGE

KANGAROO

BOOMERANG

SURFBOARD

PLATYPUS

ABORIGINAL FLAG

DIDGERIDOO

VEGEMITE

NEXT STATION CASTLE HILL

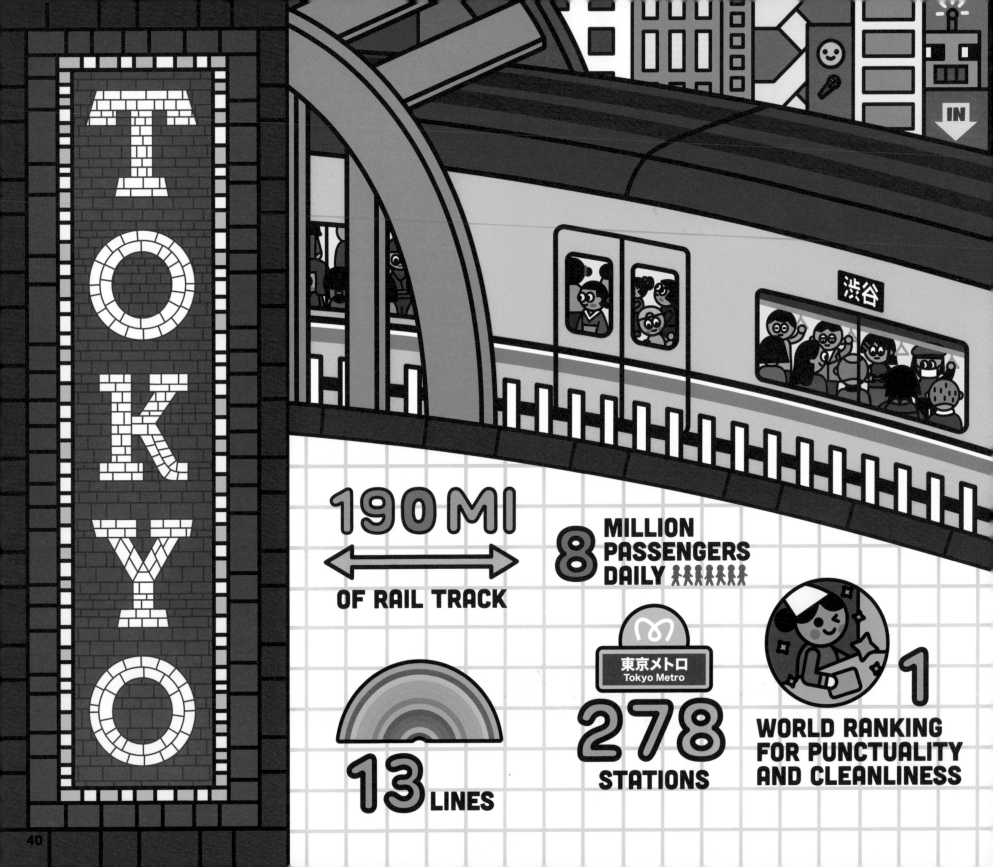

TOKYO

渋谷

IN

190 MI
OF RAIL TRACK

8 MILLION PASSENGERS DAILY

13 LINES

東京メトロ
Tokyo Metro

278 STATIONS

1
WORLD RANKING FOR PUNCTUALITY AND CLEANLINESS

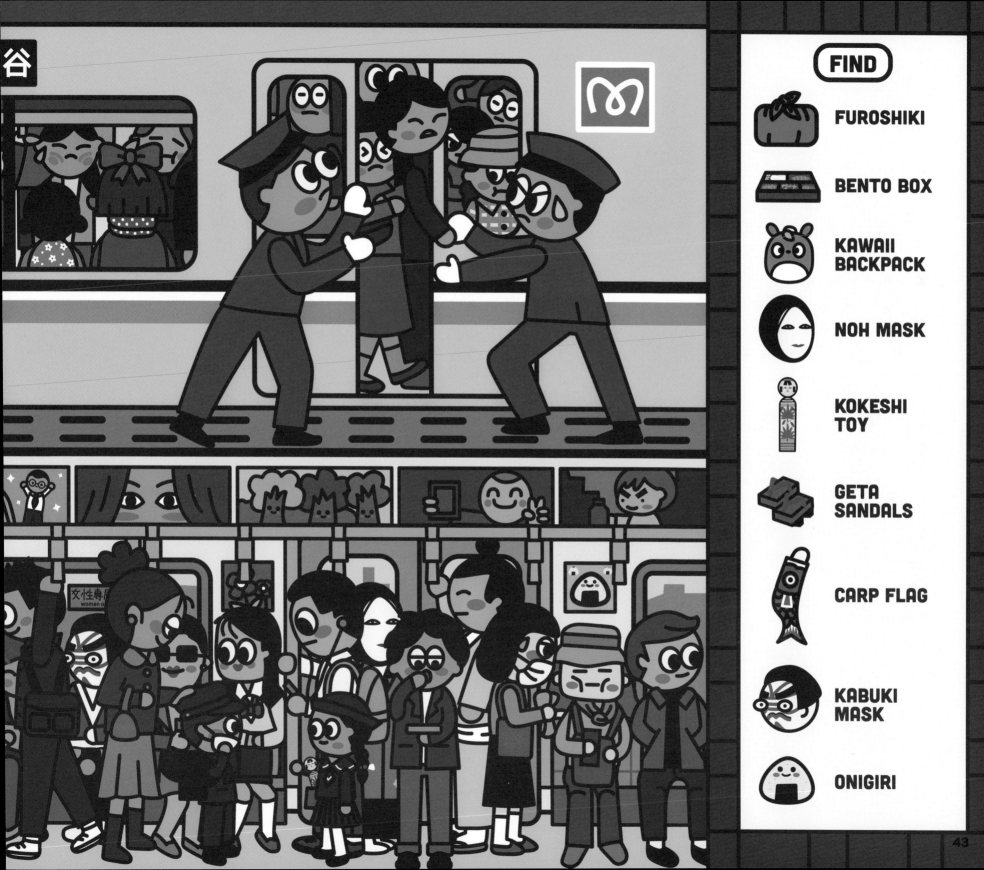

FIND

FUROSHIKI

BENTO BOX

KAWAII BACKPACK

NOH MASK

KOKESHI TOY

GETA SANDALS

CARP FLAG

KABUKI MASK

ONIGIRI

43

GLOSSARY

BEIJING, CHINA

Lion Dance
A Chinese New Year dance that brings good fortune.

Red Envelope
A gift envelope containing money.

Sun Wukong Mask
A monkey king with superpowers from Chinese legends.

Cheongsam
A traditional Chinese dress.

Jiangshi
A hopping zombie figure from Chinese folklore.

LONDON, ENGLAND

Flat Cap
A traditional British hat.

Pillar Box
A red cylindrical postbox.

British Bulldog
A dog breed with a squashed face.

MADRID, SPAIN

Flamenco
A traditional, rhythmic dance style.

Paella
A rice dish cooked in a shallow pan.

Salvador Dali
A Spanish artist famous for his surrealist paintings.

Bear & Strawberry Tree
A sculpture in the centre of Madrid.

Jamon Iberico
A leg of cured ham.

MEXICO CITY, MEXICO

Saguaro Cactus
A giant, tree-like Mexican cactus.

Lucha Libre
Masked Mexican wrestling.

Sombrero de Charro
A traditional Mexican straw hat.

Chichen Itza
Famous Mayan temple.

Papel Picado
Bunting made by cutting complicated designs into tissue paper.

Calavera
Decorated skull from Mexican Day of the Dead celebrations.

MOSCOW, RUSSIA

Double Headed Eagle
Ancient Russian symbol of empire.

Khleb-Sol
Traditional bread with salt.

Valenki Boots
Embroidered felt boots.

Matryoshka
Russian nesting dolls.

NEW YORK, USA

Big Apple
A nickname for New York City.

Pretzel
Giant, chewy pretzels are a traditional New York street food.

Playbill
A theatre magazine.

Pizza Rat
A video of a rat carrying a slice of pizza down the subway stairs became famous in 2015.

PARIS, FRANCE

Camembert
A gooey, creamy cheese.

Macaron
Two small, flavoured meringues with filling in between.

Breton Top
A stripy shirt that was originally worn by the French navy.

SEOUL, KOREA

Wedding Ducks
Carved Mandarin ducks that are given as a wedding present.

Kimchi
A side dish of fermented vegetables.

Hahoetal
Masks worn in a traditional Korean dance ceremony.

Hanbok
Traditional Korean dress.

Dol Hareubang
Large rock statues of gods.

Dobok
A Korean martial arts uniform.

Jangdokdae
Jars for preserving food.

SYDNEY, AUSTRALIA

Aboriginal Flag
The flag of the indigenous people of Australia.

Didgeridoo
An Aboriginal wind instrument.

Vegemite
A salty, black yeast spread that is eaten on toast.

TOKYO, JAPAN

Furoshiki
A Japanese wrapping cloth.

Bento Box
A lunch box with different compartments.

Noh Mask
Masks used in traditional musical-drama performances.

Kokeshi Toy
Simple wooden dolls with no arms or legs.

Geta Sandals
Traditional Japanese shoes with a wooden platform.

Kabuki Mask
Worn in Kabuki dance-drama performances.

Onigiri
Filled rice balls.